WILSON G. TURNER
AZTEC DESIGNS
Coloring Book

DOVER PUBLICATIONS, INC.
MINEOLA, NEW YORK

Note

The Aztec had their beginnings in a band of wandering peoples who followed the word of their god to the promised land of Tenochtitlán, which is now Mexico City. The Aztec conquered millions of peoples throughout Mesoamerica, and their art and culture incorporated much from those they conquered. During the fourteenth through the sixteenth centuries, the Aztec civilization dominated central Mexico. This book contains thirty black-and-white renderings of authentic Aztec designs derived from statues, ceramics, books, shields, and other priceless artifacts. Use your creativity and imagination to add your own color to these ancient motifs.

Copyright

Copyright © 2009 by Dover Publications, Inc.
All rights reserved.

Bibliographical Note

Aztec Designs Coloring Book is a new work, first published by
Dover Publications, Inc., in 2009.

International Standard Book Number
ISBN-13: 978-0-486-46779-5
ISBN-10: 0-486-46779-1

Manufactured in the United States by RR Donnelley
46779107   2016
www.doverpublications.com

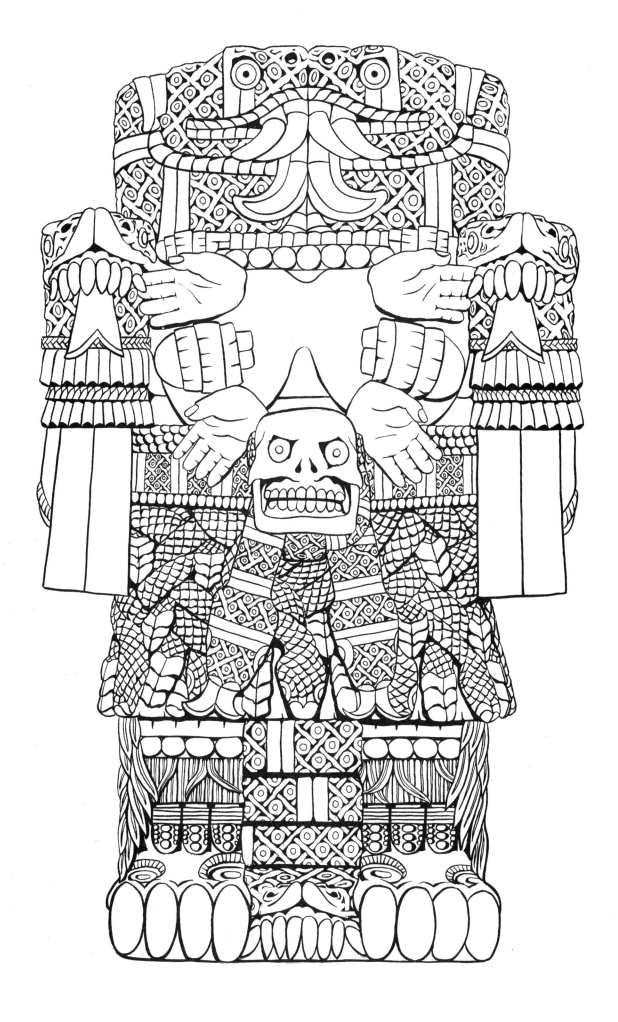

1

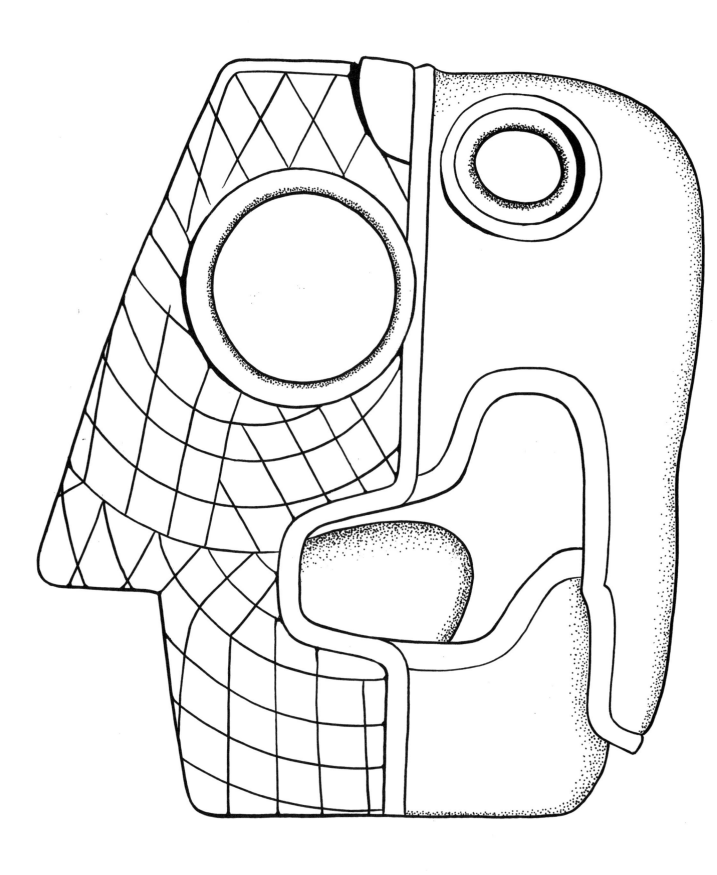

2

4

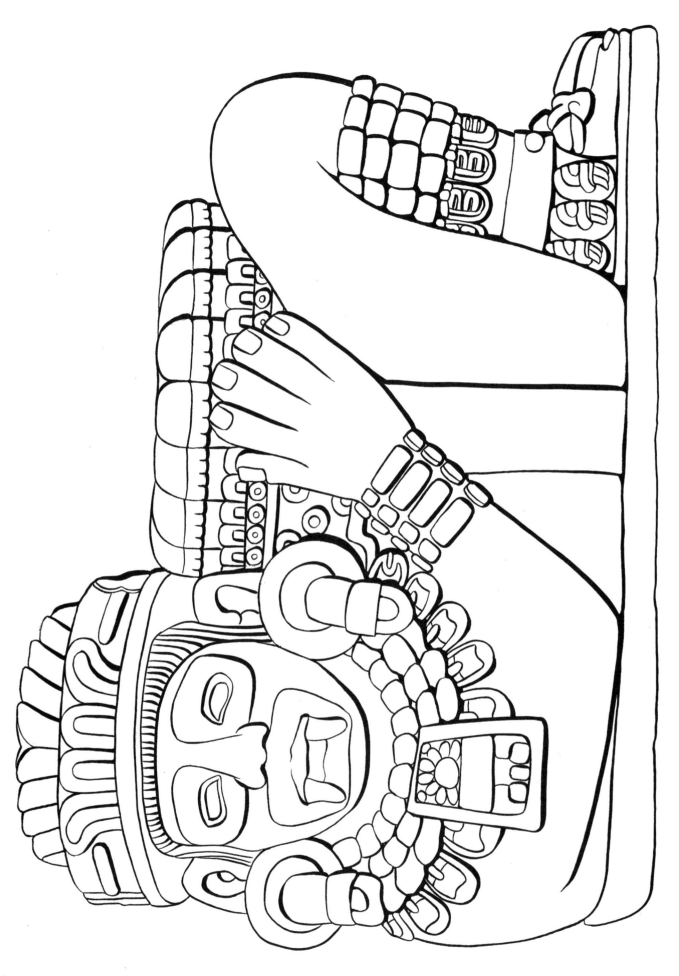

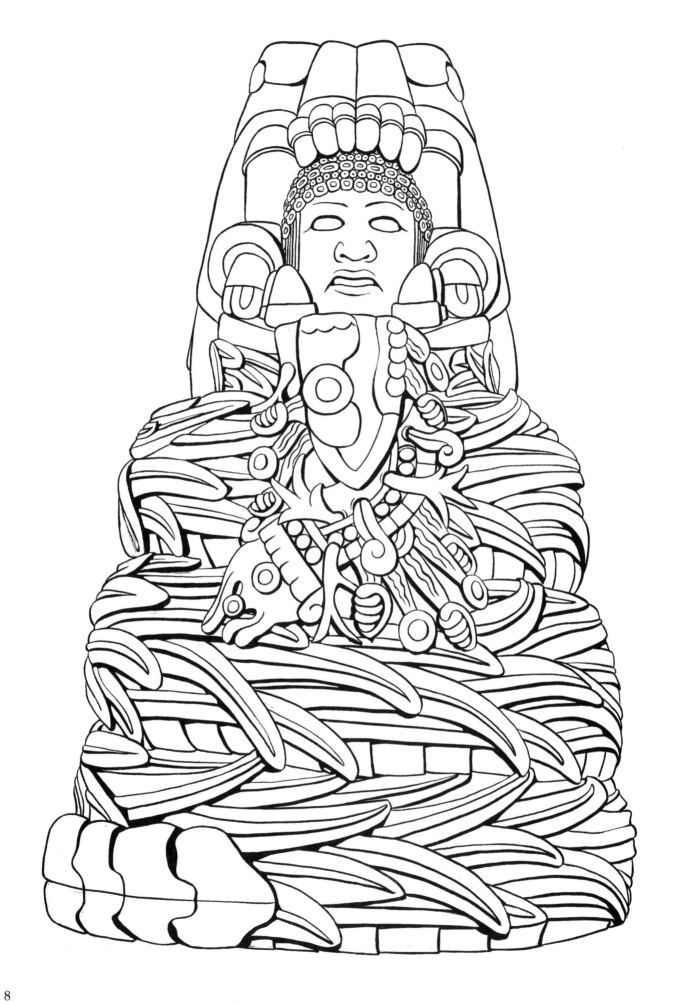

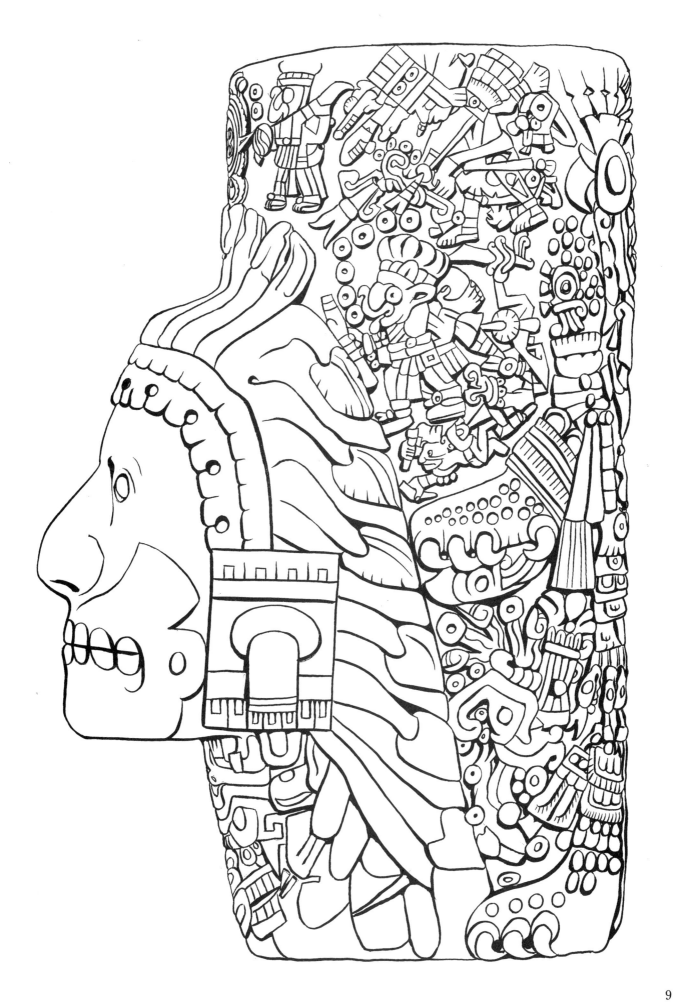

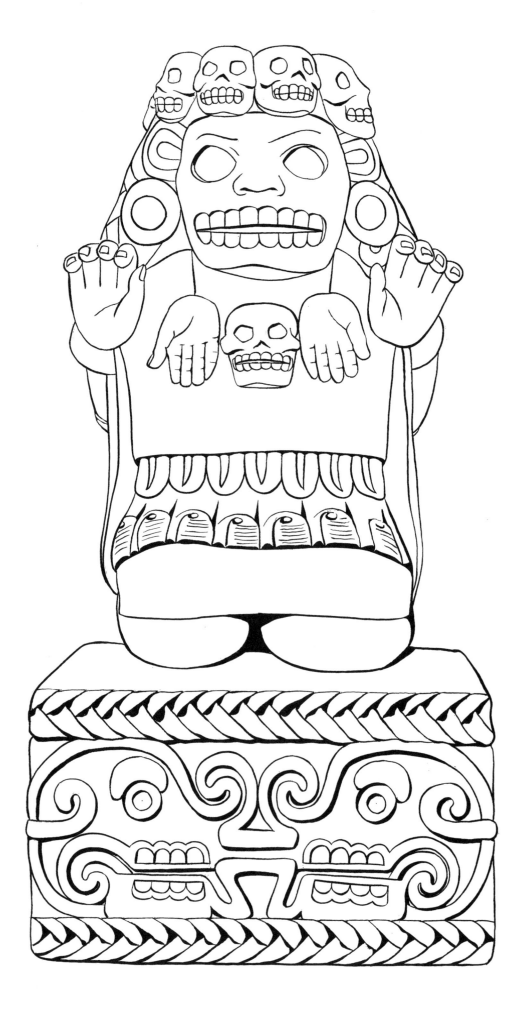

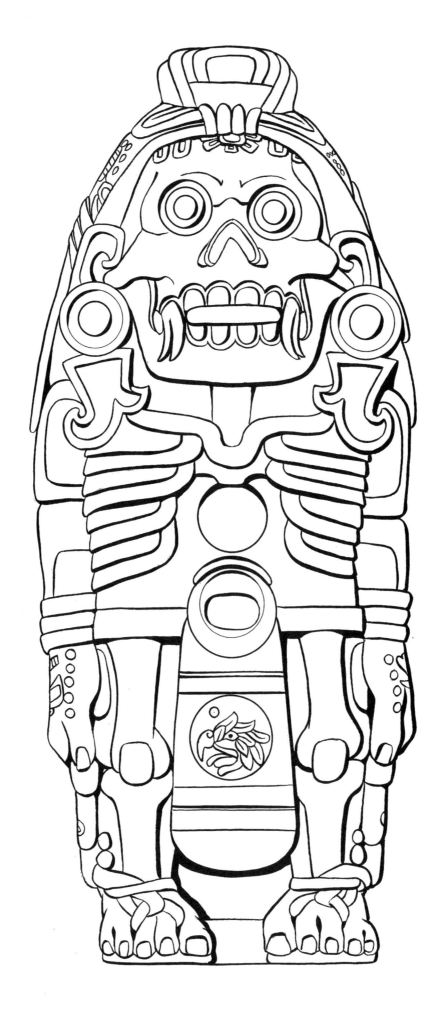

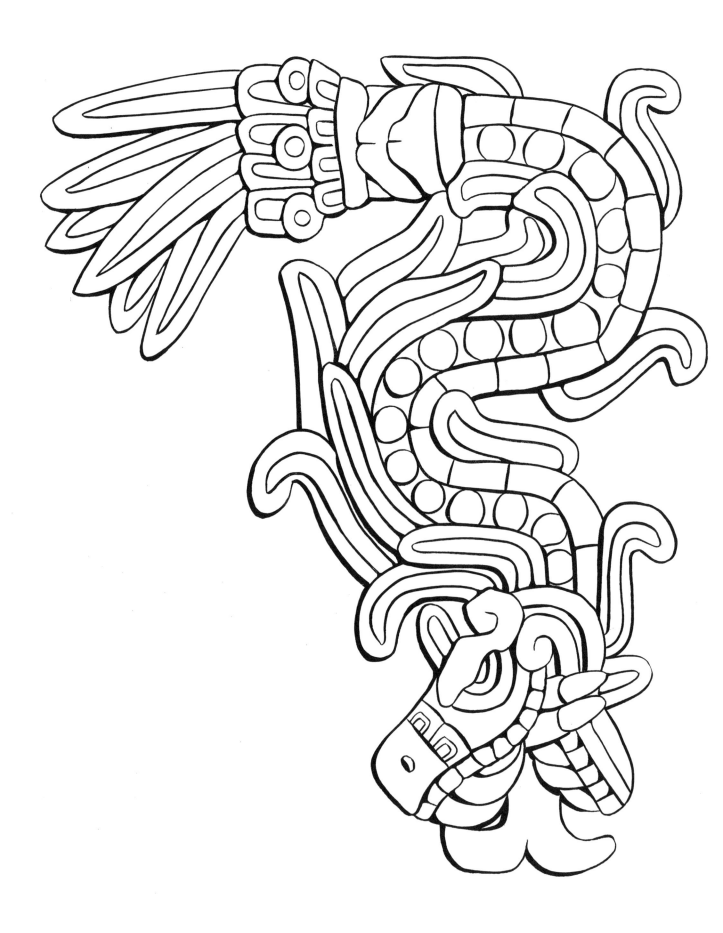